Water Gardens

A Wisley Handbook

Water Gardens

KEN ASLET, JOHN WARWICK AND JAN BOLDERS

Cassell

The Royal Horticultural Society

THE ROYAL HORTICULTURAL SOCIETY

Cassell Educational Limited
Villiers House, 41/47 Strand,
London WC2N 5JE
for the Royal Horticultural Society

First published 1977
New edition, fully revised and reset 1985
Second impression 1985
Third impression, revised, 1987
Fourth impression 1989
Third edition 1990

British Library Cataloguing in Publication Data
Aslet, Ken
  Water gardens. New ed.
  1. Water gardens
  I. Title
  635.9′674   SB423

ISBN 0-304-32000-5

Line drawings by Peter Mennim based on sketches by Paul
Cutler of RHS Garden, Wisley
Photographs by Ken Aslet and Michael Warren

Typeset by Chapterhouse Ltd., Formby
Printed in Hong Kong by Wing King Tong Co. Ltd

Cover: contrasting foliage shapes and primulas at the water's
edge.
Photograph by Michael Warren
p. 1: a pond encircled with hostas and shrubs.
Photograph by Jacqui Hurst
p. 2: the Water Garden at Wisley.
Photograph by Kenneth Scowen
Back cover: water lilies.
Photograph by Michael Warren

Contents

Introduction 7

Choosing the site 10

Stocking the pool 12

The water and its containers 16

Pond construction 22

Streams and waterfalls 28

Pumps 30

Planting aquatics 31

The bog garden 32

Maintenance 35

Propagation 37

Select list of plants 40
   Water plants 40
A. For shallow water and mud 40
B. For water 2–6 inches deep 42
C. For water 6–12 inches deep 44
D. For water 1 foot deep or more 44
E. Floating plants 45
F. Submerged aerating plants 45
G. Water lilies 46

   Bog plants 50
A. Small species 50
B. Species of medium size 52
C. Larger species 59
D. Bulbs 62
E. Ferns 62
F. Trees and shrubs 64
   Invasive plants 64

Introduction

The presence of water in the garden is a restful and relaxing sight, and also provides an opportunity to extend the range of plants grown. A water garden may be formal, but informality is more natural and is usually preferred although it is rather harder to achieve. In a rock garden setting, the movement and sound of a stream or waterfall enhance and unify the whole scene, while reflections in the pool can double the effect of flowers and foliage. Much interest is added, too, if small aquatic and amphibian creatures become established, and many of these, especially the handsome dragonflies, will often arrive of their own accord. Water plants and bog plants can extend the flowering season, particularly in the rock garden, after the early mountain plants are over, and they often have distinctive and showy colours. It is very satisfying to be able to integrate pools, stream and ditches into a general planting scheme together with the background of a boggy area, so that one type of planting merges into another, rather than having the moist places isolated.

Even a small collection of water plants can be of great educational value. Projects to restore derelict canals and village ponds, a general interest in conservation of wetlands, and the growing popularity of the aquarium, all seem to indicate a trend towards increasing interest in the subject.

Before embarking on extensive planting, try to see as many established water gardens as you can, for good ideas are always worth copying. Suggested examples are Longstock Park Water Gardens, Stockbridge, Hants (The John Lewis Partnership) where a fine collection is maintained in delightful surroundings; Sheffield Park and Wakehurst Place in Sussex, and other National Trust gardens; the Royal Botanic Gardens at Kew and also at Edinburgh: the University Botanic Garden at Cambridge; and, of course, The Royal Horticultural Society's Garden at Wisley (near Guildford, Surrey).

Read up as much as you can on the subject:
Water Gardens; *Patio Gardens*, both by Gordon T. Ledbetter (Alphabooks) are excellent and practical, though the former is the one directly related to this book. *The Water Garden* by Frances Perry (Ward Lock); *Moisture Gardening* by Alan Bloom (Faber); *The Damp Garden* by Beth Chatto (Dent); *Ponds and Water Gardens* by Bill Heritage (Blandford); and *Modern Water*

Gardening by Reginald Kaye (Faber), are also to be recommended according to taste for the subject matter, and emphasis on bog or water gardening, construction of a combination of any of them. Not all may be in print, but can be borrowed from libraries.

Other useful books are *Irises for the Water Garden* by Angela Marchant (British Iris Society), and *The Identification of Common Water Weeds*, a Ministry of Agriculture bulletin.

EQUIPMENT

Some special tools and equipment may be needed. Among others we have found the following very useful:

Nets of assorted sizes of mesh for removing floating rubbish including discarded plant material, to catch and transfer fish, and for preventing leaves from falling into the water.

Buckets are often needed when handling plants, frog spawn, fish, or removing mud and rubbish from the pool when cleaning out.

Bamboo rake. Very light in weight, cheap, and good for removing rubbish.

Hosepipe for filling the pool, siphoning or pumping it out, and for washing down when cleaning.

Stainless steel trowel which is so much nicer to use and keep clean than the usual metal types.

Waterproof boots, either as wellingtons for small pools, or thigh or waist waders for larger ones when work is to be done in the pool; also for work on the margins of larger ones because it is easier to reach up or across from within the filled pool.

Bowls for floating in the water to use instead of a bucket or trug for holding rubbish. The domestic plastic ones are ideal.

A pool of unusual shape surrounded by a colourful border of bedding plants

Choosing the site

This is a very important decision. The site should be sunny, preferably clear of trees and large shrubs, even evergreen ones. Leaves that fall into the pond break down to give off toxic gases which can be harmful to fish and other water life if in sufficient quantity. This may easily happen in a small pool.

Water plants love the sun and the stronger the light the sturdier will be their growth and the more likely they are to mature and flower freely. Shade can compensate to some extent for insufficient moisture in a bog garden in a dry season, but it may induce weak and floppy growth, which is not wanted. Shade can be used for some bog plants if only foliage is required i.e. *Rheum* spp., *Rodgersia* spp. and *Peltiphyllum peltatum*.

Rodgersia tabularis, a large bog plant with imposing leaves and astilbe-like flowers in summer

By edging this pond with stone and allowing the marginal plants to grow freely, a natural look has been achieved

The roots of some trees, particularly birch which spread, and elm which sucker, can make excavation of the pond difficult, and root growth later may cause damage to the completed pond.

When a series of pools is to be constructed, always build the lowest one first, moving upwards each time to the next pond. Make the pond large enough. Many pools are too small in proportion to the gardens around them.

One word of warning – a pond is a very attractive lure to children, just as it is for adults, but children cannot see the danger, so keep the pond covered to prevent small children from falling in.

Stocking the pool

There are many very dwarf moisture-loving plants suitable for the margins of a stream or pool in the rock garden, but the smaller the area, the more selective one must be. In the pools, too, the smaller the area, the more particular must one be not to plant things that are liable to swamp their neighbours. There are really very few species suitable for planting in the smallest pools, but they are good plants and can produce a lovely effect.

One of the most important things about a booklet on water gardens is to issue serious warnings about plants that are too invasive, and here it must be said that the descriptions in many nursery catalogues are not always helpful. Some of the most rampant weeds are sometimes included in a 'mixed' or 'beginner' collection – often, perhaps, because they are so easily propagated. An example of this is the common yellow musk, *Mimulus guttatus*, which became one of the worst weeds on our Wisley rock garden. Try to recognise the rogue from the beginning if you can: there are so many other first class plants. However, some large, vigorous plants can be quite suitable for a small pool if they are divided and replanted regularly as they get too big. Examples of this are *Iris pseudacorus variegata* (golden variegated leaves) and also the North American pickerel weed, *Pontederia cordata*, which is one of the few hardy water plants with blue flowers, which makes a very large clump in a lake. Another in this category is the lovely pink flowering rush, *Butomus umbellatus*.

As a contrast, some of the smaller floating plants that are quite in proportion in a small pool can increase much too fast, but are easily thinned out with a net or a bamboo rake (a much better tool than it looks). In a big lake they can be more difficult to keep under control unless a high wind blows them all to one side. One example is the frog-bit, *Hydrocharis morsus-ranae*, with floating leaves resembling those of baby waterlilies produced on stolons like strawberry-runners; this is fine when young and looks just right, but it can choke up the surface of narrow streams and small pools. Nevertheless it is easily controlled if regularly thinned until it forms its winter resting buds (like little bulblets), which sink to safety in the mud in autumn and reappear in spring. A surprise here is the very handsome water soldier, *Stratiotes aloides*, and many a country pond has been spoiled by well-meaning plantsmen who have thrown in a rosette or two which have increased and choked up the whole surface. In spite of this, it is still well worth planting in a small pool (but keep it well thinned out), because of its interesting habit of sinking below water in winter and rising to expose some of its rather yucca-like leaves in the summer at flowering time.

Animal life. Many animals will arrive spontaneously e.g. pond-skaters and whirligig beetles, and can appeal to those members of the family less interested in plants. Much fascinating microscopic life is also found in pond-water. Frogs, toads and newts, so useful in the garden generally, may well appear and deposit their eggs in the water. Frog-spawn can be collected and put in; also the tadpoles are good scavengers and help to keep the water clean and clear. At one stage they are vegetarian and live on the minute plants such as algae that discolour the water. The curly ramshorn snail is also effective for this but it does not reproduce very quickly. Other water-snails are less efficient, the long pointed ones being positively harmful to garden water-plants, because they eat the leaves.

Good richly coloured specimens of the common goldfish are probably the best and most effective fish for ordinary use. They are quite likely to increase if both sexes are present, but few people can tell them apart. Many are black when young and develop the golden colour when older, but some never do. Golden orfe are equally decorative and more lively, and are often more visible as they tend to feed at the water surface. They can be very long-lived and may get big. Like many plants, fish introduced when small have a better chance of becoming established. Small ones are cheaper, too, and suffer less from travelling to their new home. That little fish so popular with children, the stickleback, will live and increase in any small pool; it is a most effective birth-control agent for goldfish however, as it will gobble up all the eggs and young, so don't put them in if you want other fish to increase. Minnows need running water and do not like still pools much, but are always worth trying.

If the fish suffer from lack of air in hot summer weather, a fine water-can rose or a suitable mist jet can be fixed up on a hose to spray on to the pool and thus aerate the water. This should only be necessary with new pools. As the 'balance of life' is established, and with sufficient depth of water in relation to the surface area, shortage of oxygen should not occur.

In winter if the water is frozen for more than three days the ice needs to be broken in order to allow any build-up of toxic gases trapped by the ice to be released. Do not use a hammer as the fish may suffer from concussion! Instead, make holes in the ice at both

13

ends of the pool, by standing cans of hot water on it, and repeat this daily if necessary. Alternatively use a small electric pool heater made for the job. A little air under the ice will act as insulation (like double glazing).

Nature will not leave a small pool alone any more than it will leave an empty piece of ground unclothed with vegetation. In cultivating a garden we have to fight nature all the way. If left alone, pools and ditches would soon become choked with silt and leaves, blown or washed in, and would then become full of quite unwanted plants from seed blown in or perhaps carried on the feet of visiting water birds. Pieces of plants may also appear in this way, and the disastrous spread of *Elodea canadensis* (Canadian pondweed or water thyme) over a hundred years ago when it choked many canals, was not by seed but was entirely vegetative. Now that it has lost its expansive vigour we do use it as a submerged aerating plant, but other species are safer and better.

In spite of all these awful warnings, water gardening remains a delightful and fascinating art and it is to be hoped that more people will indulge in it and succeed with it, as they should if they are careful to use suitable plants.

Opposite: *Iris laevigata* 'Variegata', with its striking foliage and flowers, is one of the best plants for a small pool
Below: Hemerocallis, yellow flag irises and forget-me-nots in a waterside group

The water and its containers

WATER CONTAINERS

It is possible to grow aquatic plants, even waterlilies, in any container that will hold water. Half barrels have often been used, as have the large concrete rings now used for sewer pipes and septic tanks. If a cracked ring can be obtained cheaply and sunk to the rim in the ground, the bottom can be sealed with concrete, and, to seal the crack, the inside painted with an inert and harmless bitumen material. The tiny waterlily *Nymphaea pygmaea* can even be grown in a glazed kitchen sink.

Larger ponds can be bought as ready-made shaped fibreglass units with marginal plant shelves, but these are expensive. These and the shallow sinks are much more susceptible to algal problems than larger ponds because they are relatively shallow in relation to their surface area.

Liners in polythene, PVC (reinforced and non-reinforced), and butyl, are all readily available. Polythene must be black, and as temporary housing for water and bog plants can be of a thin gauge, is easy to instal but short-lived where it is exposed above ground, only lasting one or two years. The PVC liners on the other hand last longer, from 5 to 10 years; those with reinforcement are more expensive but have about 10 years life. The most expensive liner is butyl and is, unlike other liners, usually black; it has by far the longest potential life.

The best colour for liners and pools in general is black, as it reduces the growth of algae, particularly in the early life of the pool when they multiply very rapidly: aesthetically it looks so much better. Pool liners can deteriorate quickly when directly exposed to the ultra-violet rays of the sun, so they must be kept covered as much as possible by water, plants, paving, or rock garden stone.

Another method of containing water is to use concrete, but if this is to be used it must be done properly with every care taken at each stage. Plenty of time must be allowed for the actual concreting, with help available to complete the work, preferably in one day, to be sure of a watertight pool.

A compromise method which we have used at Wisley is to use concrete as a thin wall for the sides only and a butyl liner over the floor and sides, with a blanket of fibreglass between the concrete wall and liner to prevent chafing. This is ideal for most pools except the largest ones and lakes. The concrete does not have to be waterproof, and it can be laid over a period of time, and bricks or building blocks can replace concrete poured in *in situ*. The resultant pool has upright sides and the top edges can be covered with plants, turf, paving or stone for a rock garden; part of the pool can be sectioned off, filled with soil, and planted with bog plants. Most important of all, the water plants can all be grown in containers and be placed anywhere on the floor of the pool, even raised if necessary on building blocks. All this is only possible with upright sided pools, i.e. concrete sides (see below).

a

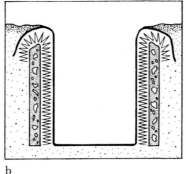

b

c

Containment for water. (a) All concrete; (b) liner covering a thin wall of concrete, with base of soil; (c) liner alone with a marginal shelf for bog plants or shallow water plants. Note the relative floor spaces for placing plants in relation to the pool surface areas of each method. For all concrete sided pools (as in (a) and (b)) angle top edge as shown; this enables the concrete to be easily disguised with soil and plants. (See p. 19 for key).

All other pools which have sloping sides limit the planting and access to the pools, to within the level bottom of the pool. Marginal shelves can be incorporated, but even if built in all the way round they do limit the height and width of the containers to be used. It has been suggested that sloping sides allow ice to rise without friction. True, but what happens to the frozen soil outside the pool? This will surely crack the concrete.

One further point that may help to decide which method and size of pool to build is that of soil type. On a fairly heavy soil, the liner should remain stable along the edges even when occasionally trodden on. However, this is not true of light or sandy soils, and a broken edge will totally spoil the effect; it also means that the water level will drop and expose more liner to break down under sunlight.

Pools for most purposes are built on the lowest ground available for fairly obvious reasons, but should one want more than one pool, then build the lowest first, and so on upwards. With such construction the liner pools are definitely easier to build with concrete walls, as one liner can overlap into the next with no loss of water, although it is perfectly feasible to build waterfall pools entirely in concrete, or liner. In all instances stone may be used to disguise the exposed liner or concrete. All soil surrounding upper pools must be contained by the stone construction with no leaks of soil, otherwise erosion takes place and the liners will move, especially those without any concrete support. Fibreglass pools are not recommended as these are hard to disguise, but can be used and very often are.

The depth of the pool is ideally not less than 2 feet (60 cm), for four main reasons. Very small and shallow ponds will heat up quickly and algae develop rapidly in water containing plenty of oxygen, which is increased every time it is topped up, and even more so when it is refilled on cleaning out operations. It also heats up very rapidly in large but shallow ponds. When fish are introduced they frequently need to escape from the glare of direct sunlight in warm weather, and from ice in freezing temperatures in winter. If the pool is shallow there is no protection in such extreme conditions. Water plants require a minimum depth (of one inch (2.5 cm) above the tops of the containers, and with a few exceptions, most require containers of 1 foot (30 cm) or more in depth. This may be impossible in shallow pools. The last criterion may not apply to all ponds, but herons can step into a shallow pool. They do not dive, but can devastate a pool, particularly by stepping on an unfilled space on a marginal shelf.

The shape of the pool is best kept very simple. Where it is made with a liner, a simple oval or circle is easy to construct and maintain. With a figure of eight or pinched kidney shape it can be difficult to fold the liner and there may be a definite weakness in the narrow waist where ice gets thick in winter, unless one end, to include the waist, is incorporated in the blocked off section for a bog garden.

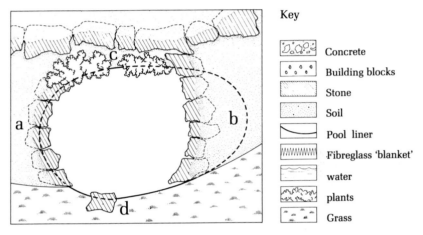

Key

	Concrete
	Building blocks
	Stone
	Soil
	Pool liner
	Fibreglass 'blanket'
	water
	plants
	Grass

Pool surrounded by (a) scree with stone edging; (b) construction of a bog section within the pool; building blocks capped with stone are used. (Dotted line indicates stone under soil surrounding the pool); (c) plants growing over pool edge; (d) turf laid to pool edge.

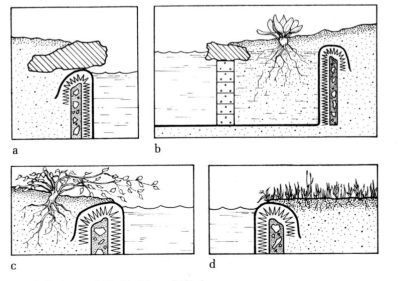

Detailed views of (a), (b), (c), and (d) above.

A concrete pool is easier to make in a series of straight lines, long or short to suit the shuttering available, with the resultant angles, and possibly some of the straight lines, blocked off as a series of bog gardens.

The puddled pool or lake is one method of construction not yet mentioned which has been used successfully on larger projects. The method entails a great deal of skill and needs a large volume of high quality clay; this is usually beyond the scope of do-it-yourself gardeners. It is described in Reginald Kaye's book *Modern Water Gardening* and needs no further mention here as the best description is given in his book.

PLANT CONTAINERS

Square plastic containers for water and bog plants are available from garden centres and sundriesmen, these have perforations in the sides as well as below. (It is unfortunate that the sides slope inward giving a top heavy container.) Plastic pots make good containers, particularly if the base sections are filled with concrete to make them more stable. Black plastic dustbins can be cut down in height, to make two or more floor containers for use in larger pools. Make sure the bases of the upper sections fit flush with the floor of the pool to prevent soil erosion, and place polystyrene sheeting underneath these and any other sharp containers to prevent cutting the liner. (see page 24). Concrete rings and wooden half barrels can also make plant containers but do be aware of the steel bands which can rust away on the barrels. Freezer cartons make excellent containers suitable for shorter plants, although the taller types may need concrete in their bases. Clay pots and particularly clay pans or half pots are heavier and therefore suitable, but again avoid the tall narrow ones which topple over too easily.

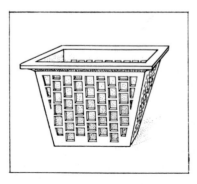

A square plastic container made specifically to hold bog and water plants, and available from many garden centres and sundriesmen.

Avoid containers made entirely of steel or iron; these will quickly rust and create a pollution problem within the pond. Thin wood, sacking and wicker work are better not used as they will very soon disintegrate.

The shallow, marginal shelves of pools are for holding bog plants, so that the plants need shallow containers. In the pool itself building blocks can be laid on polystyrene to prevent chafing and the containers mounted on them if the plant needs raising up at all.

Tall plants such as the flowering rush *Curtonus umbellatus* and pickerel weed, *Pontederia cordata*, and many others are best planted in broad containers at least a foot (30 cm) deep if the wind is not to blow them over.

Building blocks and concrete placed in containers for stability, are best coated with a bitumen paint to hide the concrete and to seal in any toxic lime within the concrete which might leach out. It is also advisable to paint plastic containers and polystyrene with black paint; this will act as camouflage.

Pontederia cordata, one of the few water plants with blue flowers

Pond construction

The simplest pools to install are the fibreglass types. Dig a hole slightly larger than the contour of the pool, remove any stones and other sharp objects, and after the pool has been test fitted with a spirit level, smooth over the entire surface area. Then re-insert using soft sand over the entire base surface area until it fits flush with the ground, or even below the ground level if there is a slight slope. Never leave the pond suspended above ground level, as it is likely to be damaged, and it also looks unsightly.

The liner pool is also fairly simple. To measure the area of liner required before starting to dig the hole, mark out the site with thick string or rope on the area outline proposed, and place thinner strings within it to gauge where and what you propose to plant, allowing for growth spread.

It is surprising how small a surface area of clear water is left. A good maxim, though by no means essential, is to allow a minimum of two thirds of clear water; by this means you can judge the size of the pool you want, then measure the maximum length, and the maximum width, and to each of these measurements add twice the depth of the pool. Some liners are of specific measurements, in which case order the size measured or larger. Others may be ordered made to measure.

Dig the hole as marked out with a 20° slope, and if required a marginal shelf can be incorporated all the way round or over part of the pool to hold shallow baskets for marginal plants; the shelves are best made 9in. (22 cm) below the rim. Check with a spirit level over the whole pool lip area. The resulting level must not be more than $\frac{1}{2}$ in. (7 mm) out to enable the pool to be filled to the brim. Remove any sharp objects and cover the whole surface area with soft sand including the lip all the way round.

Stretch the liner out over the pool carefully letting the middle touch the ground, then lower the remainder of the liner without trying to fit it exactly in all the spaces. Lay weights on the liner all the way round the lip to hold the liner in place. Begin to fill with water, and allow the folds to form naturally. There will be some elasticity, but the weights may need adjusting whilst the pool is filling where the liner is stretched too tightly. With the slight stretching of the material and the angle of slope there should be no need to allow for an overlap over the lip in extra length and width, but care must be taken to gauge this when laying it out in the first place.

There are now three possibilities with the overlap liner. If the end of the pool is to receive a waterfall, the liner can be extended upwards slightly to prevent water leakage from the pool above (see page 26); the edges of the liner may be laid flat underneath flat paving slabs on firm soil and the stones mortared onto the liner and soil and any surplus liner cut away; or the pool may be edged with grass, or a garden bed, in which case the liner can be buried 2 in. (5 cm) out from the rim by up to 6 in. vertically (15 cm). Do not sow grass seed on the edge of a pool, it is invariably washed into it by rain; use turf at the rim and sow seed behind if necessary. If a rock garden is to be incorporated into the design, stone may be mounted in the same way as plant containers as described in the previous chapter to extend it into the pool. Always lay the stones in the pool first, then outwards and upwards; it never works successfully the other way round. To do any work in the pool, empty it first, lay down boards to stand on over the liner and place polystyrene underneath all sharp objects. Do not twist feet or objects on the liner otherwise it may be damaged.

Concrete pools should last up to 50 years if constructed in one day, floor and wall together: rather less when built separately on different days. A great deal of organisation and labour is required in building a pool with this material and it is only recommended for the most enthusiastic of gardeners. However, to build a thin wall to retain the soil, leaving the floor covered in sand to insert a liner afterwards is relatively easy (see page 17). The hole is dug out to allow a wall 2 to 3 inches thick (5–8 cm) with vertical sides. If the pool is 2 feet deep (60 cm) sheets of standard hardboard, 8 feet by 4 feet (240 × 120 cm) can be cut longitudinally to give two sheets each 8 feet by 2 feet (240 cm × 60 cm) for shuttering on the inside with the soil cut straight and vertically for the outside shuttering. Overlap slightly one sheet over another and hold in position with long stakes on both sides. Use a simple concrete mixture of $\frac{3}{8}$ in. ballast (2 cm) and cement in the ratio of 8 to 1. Use some reinforcing rods or scrap metal which can be hammered into the ground (not to touch the side soil nor the hardboard) and be surrounded by concrete to just below the height of the pond rim. Drive them up to 18 inches into the ground (45 cm). Tamp in well every 6-inch (15 cm) layer of concrete, and ensure that the reinforcing is enclosed within the concrete. Fill in with the soil from the excavation to hold the hardboard on the inside at the same time. Working together in layers in this way keeps the relatively soft hardboard under even pressure, and saves the bulges produced using acrow jacks or baulks of timber and boards.

After completion and testing with a spirit level, leave to set for two days or more, then remove the soil and shuttering, and with a brick rub down the rough edges on the ridge.

The base is then cleared of sharp objects, a layer of sand put on, and the liner applied over a 'blanket' of fibreglass. The fibreglass is supplied by butyl suppliers and should cover the exposed concrete including over the ridge and down on the outside by 3 to 4 inches (7–10 cm), with the liner covering the fibreglass and floor. The liner is trimmed off to overlap the fibreglass. The liner and fibreglass end should always be in close contact with the concrete wall, regardless of what is laid on top including paving slabs. Should the liner need replacing, then the operation is easier than without a wall. There is no need to build a marginal shelf, as building blocks can be used to mount the marginal containers (see below).

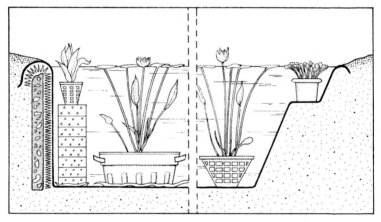

Left: a concrete reinforced liner pool in which wide containers can be used. Right: a liner pool with different types of plastic containers.

For further information on entirely concrete pools as made at Wisley, a leaflet is available. Please apply to the Director, R.H.S. Garden, Wisley, Woking, Surrey GU23 6QB.

Additional points. To ensure that the pool can be viewed closely when set in grass it would be prudent to set a stone or two on the edge of a liner-only pool as viewing platforms, to save constant pressure on the liner edges. Set the flat slabs below grass level for ease of mowing.

The more that liners can be disguised, the better they will look aesthetically and the longer the life of the liner will be. Pockets to break up any regular lines or to create areas for bog plants are purposely allowed for in vertical-sided pools, and can be made of building blocks; these should join together well for soil retention, finish below the water line when laid, and be topped with stone (preferably angular). (see below).

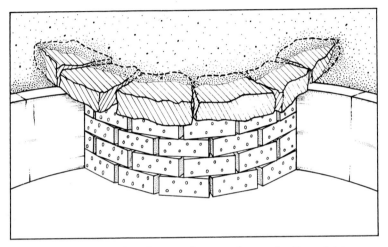

Building blocks topped with stone disguise the regular line of this pool.

The stone can also be used to extend over the edge of the pool into a bed to give a further integration with the rest of the garden when there is no rock garden. The pockets created should be filled with ordinary garden soil (e.g. excavation top soil) lower down, but definitely good soil above, which should extend above the water line, and over the pool rim to hide the liner and to give moisture outside the pool by capillary attraction. When this is done, only the pool has to be topped up with water, the plants inside and immediately outside the pool receive it automatically. Do not exaggerate the rise of soil height unnaturally (2 to 3 inches (5–8 cm) will suffice), otherwise the rain and cleaning operations will level it out into the pool!

Where a rock garden is to be constructed above the pool, use the same type of stone within the pool to make it an extension of the rock garden, and not a separate unit.

Liners for pools above a base pool should have an extension of their length allowed for to carry water from the upper to the lower pool and overlap by a good margin the overlap in the base pool (see page 26). The exit channels from each pool are best made wide and shallow, rather than narrow and deep, to avoid a sudden drop in level when the water stops flowing. Exposed pools look awful and the life of liners can be shortened.

Repairs to pools are usually a confounded nuisance, so good construction and care is important!

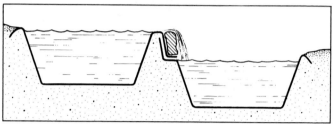

Liner pool without concrete sides shows liner extended over from lower to upper pool; a space should be allowed between each pool to ensure stability. A stone facing hides the liner and retains the soil.

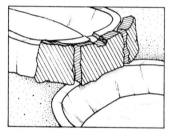

Stone to hide the upper liner is laid on building blocks and mortared to the liner with waterproofing added, to seal upper pool exit.

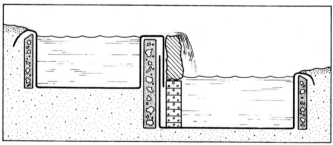

Concrete liner pools are connected in this case by a wall common to both pools.

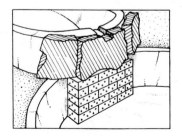

The concrete supported pools are built one to the other, and building blocks are fitted inside to carry the stone into the water.

A pool and rock garden designed as an integrated feature

Streams and waterfalls

If one is lucky enough to have a natural stream, even a tiny trickle, it can easily be dammed into a series of pools, large or small. Once the winter rains have filled them the amount of flow should continue as before, and none of the water need be wasted. A steep rushing stream is not always satisfactory unless there is a considerable and constant flow of water. A chain of pools, in effect a succession of short canals, with a waterfall from each one to the next, is more effective, and it is easier to plant both the water and the margins. (see below and opposite)

It is quite a simple matter to test the future effect by making some temporary dams, which can be made permanent later when you are satisfied with the arrangements.

If the soil is of a retentive nature, as it usually is where there is already a stream, a lining for each pool may not be necessary – just a series of dams to stem the flow until each pool brims over.

One can still achieve a natural looking stream by using a piped water supply, and it can be made very economical by using a

An effective waterfall provides an interesting focal point

A series of pools on different levels fitted into a limited space and imaginatively planted, with a clump of astilbes in the foreground

pump to recirculate the water. It is now easy to have a waterfall as there are many efficient small submersible pumps for this purpose, which recirculate the water already in use. All they need is some half-inch plastic hose for the water, and a safe electrical connection which must be undertaken by a qualified person. A waterfall need only be quite small, just enough to get a little movement. Water plants do not in general need anything but still water, and water lilies, in particular, are better with no more than a very slow current.

29

Pumps

Circulating pumps are necessary for pools in series to provide waterfalls and for fountains. (Fountains are best confined to formal pools which are not covered in this book.) There are two types of electric pump available. The simplest, and cheapest, with sufficient power for most ponds, is the submersible type, which is placed in the pool. A hosepipe then runs from the pump to the top of the series of pools. It is sensible to run the pump underneath the waterfall where ripples of water will disguise it.

The electric cable from the pump runs to the nearest convenient power point, so that the pools need to be at a reasonable distance from that point. The movement of water down a short distance from top to bottom means very little water is lost in transit from the base pool back into the same pool and therefore a very small loss in water level. The different makes and sizes of pumps will control the flow, but in addition the pipe can be pinched to reduce its diameter thus reducing the flow still further. The amount of flow is governed by the volume of water in the base pool, the distance it has to flow through the pipe from the pump, and the height of the rise from bottom to top. Waterlilies, which resent much movement of water, can be placed furthest from the waterfall to overcome this restriction in a small pool.

The second type of pump is a surface pump giving a far greater pressure, again depending on the size, distance of travel and lift. These should only be used for larger pools otherwise the waterfall may cause such a splash as to lose too much water, and reduce the chances of growing any plants at all. The chamber for the surface pump needs to be close to the pool, and preferably below the water line of the bottom pool, but this is not essential. This ensures that the pump remains primed at all times, and minimises possible starting troubles when turning the pump on again after a period of non-use. The hosepipe from the pump, if directed downwards into the top pool, will make the water appear more natural than when placed horizontally and jetting out from it.

The choice of pumps available is large. See your local stockist taking with you the information you need to choose the model. For all electrical pumps, it is essential that the electricity supply is properly fitted by a qualified electrician.

Planting aquatics

It is essential to plant firmly, as the air-filled cellular structure of water plants makes them very light in weight and liable to float. It is advisable, especially with nymphaeas, to tie, peg, or otherwise fix them down in their containers until the new roots have a secure hold on the soil. Remove all damaged and dying leaves before planting.

No special soil is needed. A good, rather heavy loam derived from old decayed turf is adequate, although good garden soil will do. No fresh manure or fertilizer should ever be used as they will encourage algae, but a little, well rotted, old manure, or spent mushroom compost at the bottom of pockets or containers, where the roots can find it later, could be helpful.

Planting is usually done in April or May when growth has started and the conditions are warming up. Plant before filling up the pond the second time except for marginals, otherwise the containers will be too heavy (or bottomless) to place in position. Cover the surface soil in pockets and containers with small gravel or shingle after planting and water the container well, or stand it in a bath of water, before placing it in the pool, so that bubbles of air do not come up through the soil and carry up dry soil and rubbish to foul the water.

Oxygenating plants are largely submerged, and have no proper root system, but are supplied in bunches. Use lead weights to hold them in the bottom of the pond. Floating plants can literally be thrown in.

Cleanliness at all times is very important as it helps to keep the water clear. When you fill the pool with a hose, it is a good idea to tie some sacking over the hose outlet to soften the force of the water so that it flows in gently. This does not reduce the flow and delay the filling as much as using a rose or jet would do.

Do not introduce fish until three or more weeks after planting in order to ensure that there is enough food available for them.

The bog garden

An area of really wet soil is very difficult to keep clean and weed-free, as one can seldom use a hoe, and hand-weeding in the mud can be a nasty, cold and messy business. So, if one has such an area, a planting of big vigorous bog plants that will resist and smother the main run of weeds may be a good solution to the problem. A very striking effect can be made in a short time with some of these large plants with huge foliage, such as gunneras, peltiphyllums and lysichitums, rodgersias, rheums and the large spiraeas e.g. *Aruncus*, senecios (ligularias) and some of the polygonums, especially *P. campanulatum*. But big plants with big leaves need a fertile soil to produce their best effect – a sort of super ground-cover – and as with all ground-cover plantings meant to subdue weeds, it is essential to start with ground absolutely free of perennial weeds and to keep it clean until the new planting takes over and prevents new weeds getting established. The soil also needs to be enriched by digging in humus to encourage full vigorous growth.

Around large pools and lakes one can arrange, if desired, for the bog borders to be quite narrow, thus reducing the area to be kept weeded, but it need not reduce the ornamental effect much, if at all, because the foliage of the plants will grow out over the pools and adjacent paths and will not look like a narrow strip at all. They will merge with the plants in shallow water at the pool's edge, so hiding any artificial edges completely. Avoid having a great width of bog garden, otherwise maintenance becomes a problem in unstable soil.

A naturally moist piece of ground can be a ready-made bog garden, once it is cleared of perennial weeds. If you do not have a place like that, you may need to add some heavy, water-retentive (clay) soil and manure, peat and compost to hold extra moisture and to provide food to encourage the luxuriant foliage of the bolder plants. Another answer is to install a watering system if possible. A sheet of cheap polythene, deep under the site and safe from digging tools, could help a lot to slow down the drainage but might need a few small perforations at the deepest points to avoid stagnation (see opposite). Do not use the outside of the pool as a bog garden unless tied in as suggested on page 25 with soil from the bog garden going over the edge of the pool area to outside the area, so keeping plants moist but not wet.

Also use the smaller pockets within the pool, but use plants with relatively small leaves, like irises and calthas, and use the large foliaged plants in the specially lined area, and the sectioned off area within the pool.

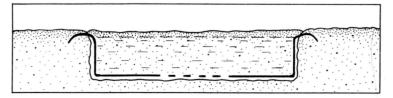

Bog plants outside a pool can be grown in a liner of polythene perforated at the base to prevent waterlogging.

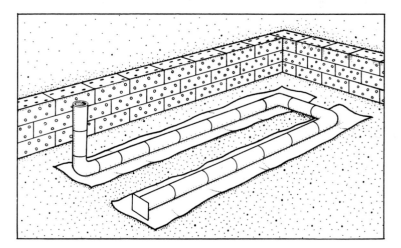

A watering system using clay pipes of 4 in (10 cm) diameter laid on top of liners laid parallel to one another but apart. The liner does not surround the site as in the upper diagram. Water is supplied through the vertical pipe.

As clay pipes have now been largely replaced by continuous corrugated plastic piping with perforations, of the same diameter, this can now be more easily accomplished.

Maintenance

When a pool has been made, filled and planted, the water will not keep clean for long but will become clouded with microscopic life. This is normal and is a stage that all new pond water must go through before it has matured and come clear again. It should do so if a good balance of plant and animal life is established in it, including especially some submerged plants to replace the oxygen used up by the fish, tadpoles, etc. It is a mistake to change the water as time will be lost, for the new water will have to go through the same stage.

Pools need regular maintenance but do not necessarily need a great deal of work at any one time until re-stocking and cleaning become necessary. Re-stocking can be delayed for much longer by observing certain criteria.

First and foremost is regular maintenance of the plants within the pool, with removal of dead and dying foliage, algae (the green slime or blanket weed which is very aptly named), and any excess oxygenators. The leaves can usually be torn off water and bog plants one at a time with a sharp tug to remove the petiole, or leaf stem, as well. The algae can be scooped up with a bamboo rake where it is thin on the surface or else using a smooth bamboo cane, twirl it with ones hands into a series of rolls. Oxygenators can be pulled out gently in handfuls. Removing the algae will give a reasonable chance for tadpoles and other creatures to keep down the small amounts remaining.

Various chemicals have been tried to control algae but they do present risks to life in the pool and are not recommended.

Choice of plants to suit the space available is also most important, avoiding unsuitable vigorous plants where space is limited.

To gain access for these operations with the least disturbance of water life, and in order to clear the pool, it is necessary to get rid of the water and keep the plants and animal life elsewhere.

Cleaning operations should not take place between March and June inclusive when fish are breeding, otherwise the females carrying eggs may be damaged and very small fry can be lost.

A delightful informal pool (above) presents a riot of colour; the stream (below) is a good example of marginal planting and makes the most of contrasting leaf shapes and forms

If a pump is available in the pond, connect a separate hose to it and pump most of the water onto the garden beds; otherwise hire a pump. The law prohibits the use of storm drains for getting rid of the water.

As the plant and animal life becomes exposed, direct the water into buckets, or a polythene liner which has been mounted between blocks, or sunk into the ground. Clean the pool using a plastic dustpan and soft brush, with a hosepipe. Do not use sharp tools for fear of damaging the liner. Keep all water plants in water, and the fish when returned to the pool must go into the same temperature of water from which they came.

Clean and re-soil the containers and follow page 31 for planting.

Netting the pool, and keeping a hole in the ice during prolonged cold weather are two jobs for the winter. Fruit cage netting is very good for a cover against most leaves, but if the leaves are small, or there are fine needle-like leaves, then use a fine gauge mesh, but do not leave it on too long, since the light into the pond will be excluded considerably, and this can affect the life in the pool, especially plants. In the bog areas in particular keep the weeds down before they go to seed to reduce maintenance. Do not leave the work until it is crying out to be done when it becomes a chore, and will have to be repeated more often than is necessary. If there is a leak in the pool there are kits available for liners of each type as well as for fibreglass pools, suitable for minor repairs. if it becomes a major problem it is probably quicker and cheaper in the end to replace the pool. For a concrete pool use a wire brush to thoroughly clean the leak area. Use a wash of cement and water over ten times the leak area and leave to dry slowly for two days. Then paint on a proprietary plastic sealant over a wider area still. If the leak or leaks are more serious, then use a liner with a 'blanket' of fibreglass over the whole pool. The water level will drop to the leak line which makes finding and repairing it easier. Lower the water still further and do the repair whenever possible from within the pool; it is so much easier.

Propagation

Aquatic plants. Almost all are propagated by division. This is usually done in April or May just when the water is warming up and the days are getting longer, the light stronger and the new season's growth is starting. This gives the plants a chance to make good growth in time for flowering and also to become well established before having to face their first winter.

Some aquatics, like *Aponogeton* and *Orontium*, are easily grown from fresh seed, which they often produce freely so that seedlings come up around the parents. The seeds can also be germinated in pots stood in shallow water and as the seedlings grow the depth of water is increased. It is a good idea to cover the seed with a thin layer of small shingle to stop the seedlings from moving about until anchored by their own developing roots.

As well as its long running shoots, *Calla palustris* develops little conical buds like bulbs, that break off and float about, and grow wherever they settle. Rhizomes of water lilies and of variegated and other water irises can be cut up into sections and submerged in shallow water to start their dormant buds and make new plants. A 'water frame' for this purpose is often a feature in gardens where a lot of aquatics are grown, and reserve plants can be kept in it to fill gaps arising in summer.

Always choose a humid day, if possible, for dividing or transplanting water plants, and never leave them exposed to sun or dry air. Keep them covered with wet sacking or other material that will not dry out and blow away as newspaper might. Do this also with plants in containers that have been put into an empty pool, while you are waiting for the water to fill it up and submerge them. A few minutes exposure to sun can do much damage to tender foliage.

Water lily roots can stain and spoil the look of your hands, especially the fingernails, for a week or more so it is advisable to wear rubber gloves when working with them.

Bog plants. Most bog plants are increased by simple division, just like any other herbaceous plants. One of the best times to divide them is April, just as young growth is starting again. Very early-flowering plants like calthas can be divided earlier or after flowering. The astilbes grow away very well if divided when the young leaves are forming.

Aponogeton distachyus, a pretty aquatic which is easily grown from seed

Lythrums are hard to divide, being woody, but are easy to root from soft cuttings in spring or summer. The variegated *Scrophularia aquatica* can be divided, but if a large number are needed, the numerous short side-shoots that form in late summer and autumn make good cuttings that are easy to root. Most irises are divided. Use seed for most of the primulas; it is the only way to raise large numbers if you have the chance and the space to plant big drifts.

Do not try to grow variegated plants from seed as they will not come true, and do not let them drop seeds into the water; the plain green ones that may come in quantity could be a great nuisance. This applies to irises, grasses, *Scrophularia*, sisyrinchiums, among others, so pick off the pods before they ripen. Another plant which should not be allowed to seed itself is the big *Alisma plantago aquatica* whose green foliage is lovely but whose progeny are legion.

Gentiana asclepiadea must be grown from seed. It is quite capable of naturalising itself in long grass – a good use for some of its abundant seed. With this, and the candelabra and other primulas, a good plan is to sow the seeds in pans in early autumn and leave them out over the winter to be frozen. If desired, they could then be taken into warm conditions in late February or

Orontium aquaticum may be readily increased from its large seeds

March to get good early plants to plant out and become established before the next winter.

The scarlet lobelias (especially *Lobelia fulgens* which is less hardy than the green-leaved true *cardinalis*) are better lifted and planted in a bed or direct in a cold-frame for the winter. Do not let them get dry. They can be divided into single crowns (or shoots) at planting time in May. Special cultivars can also be propagated in early summer by nodal cuttings.

There are a few plants among those recommended whose winter hardiness is a little suspect. The mimulus do not all look very robust, especially the highly coloured hybrids, but sometimes they will survive a very hard winter and yet succumb to a wet mild one. It is a wise precaution to root some cuttings in pots or boxes or in a cold frame in late summer and thus keep a stock under protection. A boxful or potful taken into warmth in spring will soon grow new shoots and the tips can be rooted; the process can be repeated and a large number can be produced in a short time to flower the same year.

A select list of plants

There is no dividing line between water plants and bog plants as is shown below in the list of aquatics for shallow water and mud. Some are amphibians and will climb up the bank away from the water, like *Menyanthes*, *Calla*, *Myosotis* and *Acorus*, or down into the water like many of the *Mimulus*, *Myosotis* and some of the polygonums. Neither is there a clear line between bog plants and other herbaceous plants. Hostas are very tolerant of conditions wet or dry, and lythrums are in three camps as, except in real drought, they are also excellent in a herbaceous border.

Asterisks are given to show bog and water plants which are particularly recommended – the more the better. N = British natives. By studying these lists it should be easy to pick a good selection for a small pool and its surroundings. It should be remembered that effects from foliage are just as important as those from flowers and that they usually last longer.

The depths given at the start of the sectional lists are for height between the top of the container and water level.

WATER PLANTS

Section A: For very shallow water and mud

Caltha leptosepala. Its single white flowers (April) are similar to those of *C. palustris*, but the foliage is smaller and the plant dwarfer.
Caltha palustris***. N. Marsh marigold, kingcup. One of the very best of all plants for the water's edge. April.
Caltha palustris 'Plena'******. The double flowered cultivar. An even better garden plant than the above because it is dwarfer, with a more compact habit of growth. Its flowers last longer and have more colour. It flowers in April, but as it sets no seed, it quite often blooms again later in the season.
Caltha polypetala. A giant plant, well over a foot tall, with very large rich yellow flowers, but also big leaves that need a lot of room. Not for a small pool.
Cardamine pratensis. N. Lady's smock. A pretty native of the marshes and water meadows, flowering in April. A lovely plant, but it spreads too fast in the garden, by means of fallen leaves that grow, as well as by seeds, and can become a pest.
Cardamine pratensis 'Flore Pleno'******. N. A double form which is very beautiful (also April flowering) but less rampant, although it will spread slowly by means of its own leaf cuttings.
Carex stricta 'Aurea'***. Bowles's golden sedge. A superb waterside foliage plant for spring and summer effect by the larger pool. 2½ feet (80 cm).

Carex sylvatica. N. A useful dwarf (6 inches:15 cm), non-running evergreen sedge to clothe the bank of a pool or ditch.

Carex pseudo-cyperus. N. A graceful drooping sedge. It is a non-runner, but may seed a bit too freely. Fine for the edge of a ditch or the larger pool.

Cotula coronopifolia. Brass buttons. A small, short-lived and spreading plant for the water's edge that should seed itself and give a long season of golden flowers.

Lythrum salicaria. N. Purple loosestrife. A common and showy native. It has many garden cultivars of varying heights and shades of colour and is often used in herbaceous borders. But it grows well right in the water and is very tolerant of variations in water depth. Too big for the small pool as it grows 2 to 3 feet tall (60–80 cm) and may seed itself freely.

Lythrum virgatum***. A much smaller and daintier plant, especially the cultivar 'Rose Queen' (1½ to 2 feet: 45 to 60 cm), and better for a small pool, but be sure to get the right one! (See p. 43).

Myosotis palustris******. N. Water forget-me-not. Another charming native. The cultivar 'Mermaid' is especially good, as it has larger flowers and a long flowering season, from June onwards. It may spread rather fast and is a useful filler for gaps between other plants while they are becoming established. It is easy to thin out if it becomes too prolific.

Mimulus. All the species are natives of America, flowering from July onwards, and provide us with some of the best and most colourful of all the waterside plants – ones that with a little trouble can do so much to make this kind of gardening worthwhile.

It is a pity that two of them are among our worst weeds. Let us dispose of these two first. *Mimulus moschatus* is a small yellow-flowered and rather sticky plant that will smother and choke other good plants, and should never be released on or near a rock garden. *Mimulus guttatus* is a real menace, as noted elsewhere (page 12). Its quite large and showy yellow flowers have red spots in their rather narrow throats, but not usually on the petals. It will seed profusely and smother all other dwarf plants. Avoid it at all costs. The variety *langsdorfii* is smaller, but seems no better.

Mimulus luteus. Often botanically confused with *guttatus*, for whose faults it gets a lot of the blame, but it is a much better garden plant. It does *not* have spots in the wide throat, but may have quite large and conspicuous red-brown blotches of varying sizes on the petals. It is sometimes given the strange English name of bloody drop emlets. It is probably a parent of some of the good garden hybrids.

Carex stricta 'Aurea', an excellent foliage plant for the water's edge

Mimulus cardinalis.   Grows up to 2 feet high (60 cm). The best forms are brilliant orange-scarlet, but there are other shades of red and even yellow. The flowers are of a characteristic pinched-in shape. It sets abundant seed, but it is not a nuisance as it forms a tight clump at the base of the shoots.

Mimulus lewisii.   18 to 24 inches (45–60 cm). Of simil'ar growth and one of the glories of wet places in the State of Washington. It can vary in colour from pale and washy pinks to a vivid purplish red. Its best garden value is provided by the hybrid 'Bartonianus', which sets no seed and goes on flowering all the summer. Propagate it by division or basal cuttings in spring.

Mimulus ringens.   One of the very few aquatics with blue(ish!) flowers. It does well in shallow water. It is difficult to keep, but only because when not in flower it looks so much like a willow herb that it is often pulled out by mistake.

Mimulus burnetii.   Said to be a hybrid of *M. cupreus* and *M. luteus.* 4 to 5 inches tall (10–13 cm). A good dwarf, hardy, and a persistent plant of bright coppery orange flowers.

Mimulus hybrids and cultivars.   'Whitecroft Scarlet' has for long been one of the showiest and most popular; it is dwarf with brilliant-coloured flowers. There are many others, e.g. 'Bee's Dazzler' and 'Scarlet Bee', and crimson ones like 'Red Emperor' that comes true from seed. 'Canary Bird' is a very refined yellow. 'Ochrid' is 6 to 9 inches tall (15–22 cm), with rich brown and yellow flowers; very hardy. 'Shep' is a chance seedling found at Wisley that has proved a first-class plant.

There are many others, but they may be difficult to get as few commercial firms seem to stock many kinds. Seedsmen have long offered a strain called Queen's Prize for bedding, and these, with their rather gaudy blotched flowers, are well worth trying as a cheap source of plants for a quick fill-up.

Section B: For shallow water 2 to 6 inches deep (5–15 cm)

Acorus gramineus 'Variegatus'****.**   A little aroid that looks like a pretty, dwarf iris. It is sometimes grown as a house plant, but is perfectly hardy; it is better in shallow water than in the mud on the bank. An ideal evergreen marginal plant, growing to 6 or 8 inches high (15–20 cm).

Alisma natans.   A tiny creeper for shallow water, with floating oval leaves and occasional white flowers in July.

Calla palustris***.**   This has glossy foliage, with white arum-like flowers in July and August and sometimes clusters of red fruits; it grows to 4 or 5 inches high (10–13 cm).

Iris laevigata****.**   The best of all hardy water irises, and grows well right in the water. One of the very best of all plants for a small pool, growing to about 1½ feet (45 cm). There are white and bi-coloured cultivars, but the type, a brilliant blue, is the finest, except perhaps for the superb cultivar with silver variegated leaves. All flower in June and July and at intervals later. There is also a probable hybrid called 'Rose Queen' (July and August) which is a bit dull; 2 feet (60 cm.) (See p. 15).

Iris pseudacorus 'Variegata'****.**   N. A much bigger plant (3 feet) (90 cm) and very showy, but still fine for the small pool if divided in time. The leaves become green in mid summer, but the full variegation returns in spring and is grand from the day the foliage emerges from the water until the yellow flowers fade away at the end of July. Do not let it seed as it will not come true.

Iris versicolor (blue) and var. kermesina (reddish purple).   Both are good for the water's edge, but the broad clumps are too big for a small pool. 1½ to 2 feet (45–60 cm). Flowers in June and July.

Juncus effusus spiralis.   N. Corkscrew rush. A curiosity that is of no great ornament! 9 to 12 inches (23–30 cm).

Menyanthes trifoliata, above, grows well in marshy ground or shallow water; *Lythrum virgatum* 'Rose Queen', below, produces elegant slender spires in summer

Potentilla palustris. N. An interesting and unusual native with dusky crimson flowers.

Ranunculus lingua 'Grandiflora'. N. Great spearwort. The big and fleshy handsome water buttercup that spreads too fast, but is fine if it can be confined. 2 feet (60 cm). Flowers from July onwards. (See p. 64).

Spartina pectinata variegata. A vigorous grass with a golden variegation; it needs a lot of room. 2 feet (60 cm).

Typha minima**. A dainty little reedmace with velvety heads like round drumsticks in September and October. Often it is not easy to establish. 1 foot (30 cm).

Section C: For water 6 to 12 inches deep (15–30 cm)

Acorus calamus 'Variegatus'****. Sweet flag. A variegated plant with a lot of colour in its iris-like young leaves which later get rather tall. Satisfactory in a small pool if controlled. It is not evergreen. 2½ feet (75 cm).

Cyperus longus*. N. Galingale. A graceful dark green sedge that spreads slowly but strongly; a good stabiliser of banks for ditches and large ponds. The frequent division it would need in a small pool is a tough job, but it is well worth growing. It is fine to cut for flower arranging. 18 to 20 inches (45–48 cm).

Glyceria aquatica variegata (spectabilis). A large showy and vigorous variegated grass, of which the young growth is especially pretty, with its many colours. But it is very rampant and best isolated. 2 feet (60 cm).

Menyanthes trifoliata****. Bog bean. This plant gets its name from its leaves, curiously like those of broad beans, and which are one of the food plants of the elephant hawk moth larvae. The fringed white flowers develop at the end of May from pretty pink buds. These buds form before the winter, and flowering shoots can be transplanted to keep the plants compact. (See p. 43).

Orontium aquaticum******. Golden club. This is one of the best of all aquatic plants. An aroid with no spathe, but yellow and white spadices in May. The lovely leaves are waxy and curiously unwettable. It is easily increased from its large seeds and can be divided, but this is a tough job. 9 to 10 inches (23–25 cm). (See p. 39).

Pontederia cordata*****. Pickerel weed. One of the very few blue-flowered aquatics for late summer. It makes big clumps, but is easily divided for the small pool. 2 to 2½ feet (60–75 cm). Deep green spear-shaped leaves and blue flower spikes. (See p. 21).

Scirpus tabernaemonta zebrina. Zebra rush. Tall (3 to 4 feet: 0.9–1.2 m) and handsome, this rush is not very robust. Occasional stalks that revert to plain green need to be removed.

Zantedeschia aethiopica. Arum lily. It is much hardier than one would expect a South African to be, and is a superb water plant with just the right foliage. Flowers from July to September. There are cultivars like 'Crowborough' which are shorter and these will succeed in the moist border, but many of the ordinary greenhouse ones do well if planted deeply, especially in water. It is easy to propagate from seed as well as by division. 2 to 2½ feet (60–75 cm).

Zizania latifolia. Rice-grass. Grows big, iris-like foliage for the lake-side making a handsome plant, but it never seems to flower. 2 feet (60 cm).

Section D: For water 1 foot deep (30 cm) or more

Aponogeton distachyus******. Cape bondweed, water hawthorn. The flowers are waxy white with black stamens, and sweetly scented. It sometimes seeds itself freely, even in deep water, but the small tubers are easily thinned out. The flowers rest on the surface among the floating leaves, and are produced throughout the year. (See p. 38).

Butomus umbellatus***.** Flowering rush. Tall, slender and beautiful. Leaves 18 to 20 inches long (45–48 cm); flower-stems 3 to 3½ feet (9–100 cm) with umbels of delicate pink, 3-petalled flowers in July.

Nymphoides peltatum. N. Buck bean. Has lovely well-marked floating foliage, and delicate cup-shaped fringed yellow flowers, standing a few inches above the leaves and produced from July on. But it is too rampant to be safe unless effectively isolated; probably best in a small pool on its own or with a few vigorous irises that can hold their own and not get smothered.

Polygonum amphibium. N. This does best in deep water, but it is rampant and a great pest on land, where it never flowers! The flower-spikes, 2 to 3 inches long (5–8 cm), above the floating leaves make it worth growing if well isolated. Flowers in August and September.

Sagittaria sagittifolia. N. Arrowhead. Has handsome arrow-shaped leaves and spikes of 3-petalled white flowers from July onward. The British one has a purple centre to each flower, whereas the flower-centre of the larger S. *latifolia* is yellow. There is a double *Sagittaria* (*japonica flore pleno*) that increases only slowly. The others, with their underwater rhizomes ending in 'duck potato' tubers, increase too fast and are a bit overwhelming, but are fine if isolated or at the side of a lake. 1 to 2 feet (30–60 cm).

Sparganium. N. Bur reed. Interesting as wild plants but all species are a menace in the water garden as they spread too fast – yet they are often listed in catalogues.

Typha stenophylla. N. Reed mace. This species is not so overwhelming as the great *T. latifolia*, which is no garden plant. 3 feet (0.9 cm).

Section E: Floating plants: just throw into the water

Azolla filiculoides. Floating water moss for small pools only.

Eichhornia crassipes. Water hyacinth. Tender, but worth putting out for summer for its curiously interesting structure. Don't expect it to flower out of doors.

Hottonia palustris****.** N. Lovely submerged foliage, and pale lilac flower-spikes like dainty candelabra primulas in May and June.

Hydrocharis morsus-ranae. N. Frogbit. Flowers are green and white in July.

Stratiotes aloides. N. Water soldier. Produces handsome submerged rosettes of spiny leaves. Regular control is necessary; do not put it in a big pool or canal. Flowers in July and rosettes rise to the surface.

Section F: Submerged aerating plants: for foliage effect only

Callitriche verna. N. Water starwort. A few plants are useful in the deeper water for their clear bright green foliage.

Ceratophyllum demersum***** N. Hornwort. Good feathery underwater foliage; brittle and easily controlled.

Elodea crispa. Later, better, and easier to control than E. *canadensis*.

Fontinalis antipyretica. N. Water moss. A true moss that grows well even in fast flowing water. It will tolerate shade and can be a long-lived aquarium plant. Tie to a piece of rock when planting.

Hippuris vulgaris. N. Marestail. The true marestail is best in deep water in a container; otherwise it spreads too fast. Not to be confused with equisetums (horsetail) some of which are among the garden's worst weeds.

Miriophyllum proserpinacoides. Parrot's feather. Very beautiful bright green feathery foliage, most of which comes above the water. Very fast-growing, but easily reduced. It can be pushed back under water when it gets too big and is soon up again. It is ideal for hiding unsightly edges of pools. Rather tender, so some could be kept in water indoors over winter, where it makes a pretty house plant. **M. spicatum.** N. Water milfoil. Brown feathery foliage. Not recommended because it is too rampant and rather dull.

Section G: Water lilies (nymphaeas)

These are real garden aristocrats, and in a sense the whole planting of the bog and water garden centres around them. Their needs are simple, for all they want is full sun, some good plain soil to grow in, and an adequate depth of water; 15 to 20 inches (19–42 cm) of water is plenty for all except the very big ones. Many of the less vigorous ones will do quite well with just a foot of water over their crowns, as long as we are prepared if necessary to divide them, or at least to thin them out if and when they become overcrowded. Established plants should flower from mid-June onwards.

Good catalogues will offer many more kinds than we can describe here. We have not grown every sort, but there is a wide range for you to try if you have room, and a chance to be adventurous with them.

There is one frequently offered cultivar that we do not feel that we can recommend, and this is 'Colonel Welch' which we consider a poor plant.

The following is a short list of well-proven sorts.

For very shallow water – up to 6 inches deep (15 cm) in small bowls, sinks, troughs or other containers.
Nymphaea pygmaea. A tiny, frail-looking miniature with almost translucent white petals and a rich golden centre. It often sets abundant fertile seed that germinates freely in water. The seedlings are so small and delicate that they need careful attention; they are easily smothered, especially by blanket weed.

'Helvola' is a rather stronger miniature with soft yellow flowers. It has beautiful foliage heavily mottled with rich brown, as do most of the yellow nymphaeas and their hybrids. It may be propagated by careful division, but not by seed.

'Rubra' or 'Rubis' is a tiny, deep red cultivar, akin to the preceding two miniatures. Even if it still exists, it is rare and will probably be very expensive.
Note: There is much confusion in the literature over the exact names and affinities of these three very small nymphaeas. If you wish to obtain them, it is best to see them growing and flowering first, and so be sure of what you are purchasing, and of whether they are what you really want.

For water 9 to 24 inches deep (23–60 cm)
Nymphaea 'Froebelii'. Crimson flowers; an older favourite and very popular, often the first choice for a small garden pool. Free-flowering with neat foliage.
Nymphaea laydekeri. Plants in this group of hybrids are always in great demand for the small pools. 'Fulgens' is one with crimson flowers and in many respects similar to 'Froebelii', 'Lilacea' equally neat and free-flowering, and of a light mauve-pink colour. 'Purpurata', another colour variation in this group, crimson-purple with whitish shading on the petals.

For water 1 to 3 feet deep (30–90 cm)
'James Brydon'. Probably the best all-purpose water lily. It is tolerant of various depths of water, and it will also put up with a little shade. It has huge globular flowers of a rich rose-pink and handsome circular dark leaves.

Nymphaea 'Escarboule' above, one of the most popular and reliable water lilies; and N. 'Gladstoniana', below, which has enormous fragrant flowers

N. marliacea 'Chromatella'. Large, soft-yellow flowers that remain open later in the day than most other sorts, and is therefore especially useful. The foliage is handsomely marbled, as with most other yellows, and the plant will succeed well even in partial shade.

'Rose Arey'. A dainty and high-class plant, with flowers of a rich soft pink.

'Masaniello'. An old sort, reliable and lovely. The deep pink and cream colour deepens as the flower ages. (See cover picture).

'Vesuve'. A good rich red.

'William Falconer'. The darkest crimson of all, and its leaves are also dark and handsome.

For water 2 to 4 feet deep (0.6–1.2 m)

'Escarboucle'. Large, rich red flowers. The best seller, because of its colour, size and reliability; its popularity often makes it scarce and highly priced. (See p. 47).

'Sunrise'. The best, largest, and most richly coloured of all the yellows.

Vigorous sorts for big lakes

N. marliacea 'Carnea' and 'Rosea'. Two very similar sorts, of pale delicate pink. Probably now the commonest lilies in general cultivation. Rather disappointing in colour, especially in their first year when the flowers can be almost white.

'Gladstoniana'. A huge, vigorous white, probably best in very deep water; enormous flowers with fine golden centres. If put in shallow water, the big leaves become too crowded and push each other up out of the water, which spoils the effect. (See p. 47).

N. alba. The native wild species; pure white with golden centres. Best in large ponds and lakes.

Several plants known not to be hardy can create extra interest if put into the pool for the summer. The water hyacinth (*Eichhornia*) floats with the aid of curious spongy bladders like water-wings. It increases very fast and on that account is a menace in tropical countries where it is a prohibited plant. The water chestnut (*Trapa*), if uncooked ones can be obtained, makes very handsome rosettes of floating leaves; they must be kept wet if stored. A curious mesh of finely divided submerged leaves as well as spongy, bladder-like petioles support the plants in the water.

A water garden scene

BOG PLANTS

Section A: Small plants

Ajuga reptans****. N. There are several cultivars with variegated or coloured leaves, such as 'Burgundy Glow'. Flowers in May with blue spikes up to 6 inches (15 cm).

Alchemilla conjuncta. N. Lady's mantle. Green flowers in July, and dark green foliage silvered underneath. 3 to 4 inches (7.5-10 cm).

Alopecurus pratensis 'Variegatus'. N. A golden meadow foxtail grass. Cut back after flowering and don't let it seed. 6 to 15 inches (15–37 cm).

Astilbes****. Various species and hybrids produce their spiky, feathery flower heads from May to September.

Astilbe simplicifolia has bronze foliage and creamy flowers on stems 6 inches tall (15 cm) in July and August. There are several hybrids of this growing to 1 foot (30 cm): 'Atrorosea' rich red; 'Delicata' pink and upright; 'Elegans' graceful, pendulous pink flowers; 'Bronze Elegance' dark foliage and pale pink flowers.

Astilbe × crispa 'Perkeo' is one of a group of very neat dwarf cultivars: it has pink flowers and grows to 6 inches (15 cm).

Carex morrowii 'Variegata'**. A dwarf and colourful sedge, and a non-runner, grows to 6 inches (15 cm).

Astilbe × crispa 'Perkeo', a small but striking example of these most useful bog plants

Dicentra eximea****. Delightful ferny foliage; dainty and graceful drooping pink flowers for many months starting in May. A common, but good garden plant; 9 inches (23 cm).

Dodecatheon spp.****. American cowslip, shooting stars. These lovely plants are not grown as much as they should be; flower in early summer; 9 to 12 inches (23–30 cm).

Gentiana pneumonanthe. N. Marsh gentian. A native autumn-flowering gentian, which is easily raised from seed. 6 to 9 inches (15–23 cm).

Hakenochloa macra******. A dainty and graceful grass. Its variegated cultivar is one of the finest of all ornamental grasses. 6 to 8 inches (15–20 cm).

Heloniopsis breviscapa***. An unusual Japanese member of the Liliaceae which sometimes propagates itself by producing plantlets on its leaf-tips; pink flowers in May; 6 inches (15 cm).

Holcus mollis 'Variegata'. N. Variegated Yorkshire fog. A much underrated, but useful grass; shows up in the dusk when most other colours are not visible. 6 to 9 inches (15–23 cm).

Hosta*. There are a large number of different sorts and sizes producing attractively shaped leaves of green, blue-green and sometimes variegation. Many are ideal for the waterside; they appreciate the extra moisture, but are very tolerant of varied conditions. (See p. 54).

Iris chrysographes***. Like a small refined *I. sibirica*. Flowers are prettily pencilled with gold; colours range from white and shades of blue to an almost black purple. 1½ feet (45 cm).

Iris innominata. The species is for acid soil only, but its Western Pacific hybrids are more tolerant of limy soil; 6 inches, flowering in June (15 cm).

Iris sibirica 'Perry Pygmy'***. A dwarf blue iris, flowering in June; 1½ feet (45 cm).

Lysimachia nemorum. N. Wood pimpernel. Dainty yellow flowers in June; a lovely little ground-cover.

Lysimachia nummularia 'Aurea'****. N. Creeping Jenny, with golden leaves which are bright throughout the summer, with golden flowers in July.

Mimulus spp. See under Water Plants (page 41).

Molinia coerulea 'Variegata'****. One of the finest waterside grasses, it makes compact clumps and is not a runner. It is also decorative in winter if not cut down.

Parochetus communis looks like a creeping clover until its dazzling electric-blue pea flowers appear in November. A wonderful winter flowering plant for the floor of a cold greenhouse, it will also grow outdoors in a sheltered wet corner. Encourage it to grow through some rock chippings or shingle that will give it some protection from frost.

Polygonum affine*****. Although this is often rather despised as a rock garden or border plant, it is ideal for the waterside. Don't cut it down as its browned flower heads provide winter colour. It has two good cultivars; 'Darjeeling Red', and the paler, but more compact 'Donald Lowndes', flowering in autumn.

Pratia angulata*. A little creeping plant giving double value with its white lobelia-like flowers all summer, and round purplish fruits all winter. Tolerates some shade.

Primula denticulata*****. The drumstick primula. Very early flowering, and strong-growing; various shades of mauve and purple, reds and good whites. Very special ones of good colour can be maintained by propagation from root cuttings. 6 to 9 inches (15–23 cm).

Primula rosea******. A glorious early-flowering bog plant; rich rose-pink, flowers in April. 4 to 6 inches (10–15 cm).

Pulmonaria saccharata (picta). Jerusalem cowslip, lungwort, soldiers and sailors. Early pink and blue flowers; good showy foliage. 6 inches (15 cm).

The variegated cultivar of *Hakenochloa macra*, above, a very decorative grass for the waterside; the mat-forming *Parochetus communis*, below, may be killed back by frost but usually revives

Saxifraga fortunei***.** Good foliage, and masses of dainty white flowers in October. 6 to 8 inches (15–21 cm).

Spiraea digitata nana**.** A delightful and dainty dwarf pink meadowsweet. 9 inches (23 cm).

Tiarella cordifolia.*** Foam flower. Gives a charming effect if running down a wet bank towards the water. 6 inches (15 cm). *T. wherryi* is a larger species with better foliage. 8 inches (21 cm).

Trollius pumilus. Globe flowers have buttercup-like flowers in June–July. This is a dwarf version which grows to 4 to 6 inches (10–15 cm).

Section B: Plants of medium size

Acorus calamus 'Variegatus' (see page 44).

Acorus gramineus 'Variegatus'*** (see page 42).

Arum italicum 'Pictum'***.** The best of all winter foliage; dark green freely mottled with white, 9 inches tall (23 cm).

Alchemilla mollis. Big soft-green leaves, and yellow-green flowers in summer; a fine ground cover for naturalising. 9 inches (23 cm).

Anaphalis margaritacea. N. Mountain everlasting. White flowers in autumn, and narrow grey-green leaves. 1 foot (30 cm).

Astilbe spp.****.** One of the showiest and most important genera for the bog garden. In great variety, and especially useful are the dwarfer sorts, such as 'Fanal,' 'Gertrude Brix' and 'Gloria'. They like it wet, but their crowns must be above water level, as they will not stand more than a few days of complete flooding. Reds, whites and pinks; 1 to 3 feet (30–90 cm).

Bergenia spp. Large evergreen ground-covering foliage; early, heavy heads of pink, red or white saxifrage-like flowers on 6 to 9 inch stems (15–23 cm).

Brunnera macrophylla. Big heart-shaped leaves, and 'forget-me-not' flowers, of bright blue, in May–June. 12 to 18 inches (30–45 cm).

Carex stricta 'Aurea' (see pages 40 and 42).

Filipendula palmata**.** The best raspberry-red cultivars are very choice; the white one is poor, not a good clean colour. Flowers in July on stems up to 2 feet (60 cm).

Filipendula ulmaria 'Aurea'. N. One of the meadowsweets, but with fine golden foliage; lovely for moist banks. 2 feet (60 cm).

Filipendula ulmaria 'Variegata'. N. It is a handsome plant, but has a tendency to revert to plain green.

Gentiana asclepiadea**.** Willow gentian. Rich blue and occasionally white, flowering in late summer. It tolerates some shade, and often seeds itself. 15 inches (37 cm). (See p. 54).

Geranium phaeum. Black or dusky cranesbill. There are many variations of black, purplish pink and white flowers in this species, flowering in May–June and growing 15–18 inches (37–45 cm).

Geum rivale. N. Water avens, Granny's bonnet. Two old, but good cultivars are 'Jeannie Ross' and 'Leonard's Variety'; coppery pink. Flowering in May–June. 1 foot (30 cm).

Hemerocallis spp. Day lily. There is now a wide range of cultivars, with flower colours in the yellow, orange to pink range. They are very robust, long-lived and trouble-free; they like moisture, and most of them need a lot of room. Flowering from July onwards; 2 to 3 feet (60–90 cm). (See p. 55).

Bergenia cordifolia, above, flowers in spring; *Filipendula ulmaria* 'Variegata', below, with distinctive yellow markings on the leaves

The gracefully arching stems of the willow gentian, *G. asclepiadea*, above; *Hosta fortunei* 'Marginato-alba', below, a magnificent variegated plant for sun or shade

Like all the day lilies, *Hemerocallis* 'Red Admiral', above, appreciates moisture and makes good ground cover; *Physostegia virginiana*, below, prefers full sun and will form dense clumps

Iris foetidissima. N. Its shiny winter foliage is invaluable, as so few bog plants are evergreen. The orange seeds at Christmas are an added bonus, but the flowers are rather dull. 15 to 18 inches (37–45 cm). There is a form with variegated leaves, which is less vigorous and flowers less freely.

Iris kaempferi. Clematis iris. The superb large Japanese iris which likes acid soil. Do not plant right in the water, but the roots need to be able to reach it. The flowers are flatter than other irises, and are produced in June; 1½ to 2 feet (45–60 cm).

Iris sibirica. A wide range of cultivars. Very slender in leaves and flowers; in blue or white and some other colours. Grows to 2 to 2½ feet (60–75 cm).

Lobelia cardinalis. Bright scarlet flowers, with green leaves. From Canada and northern U.S.A. Flowers in July–August. 2 feet (60 cm).

Lobelia fulgens**.** Scarlet, with purplish red leaves; from southern U.S.A.; not so hardy as *L. cardinalis*. 'Queen Victoria', 'Huntsman' and 'Bee's Flame' are good cultivars. Some hardier hybrids have recently been developed in Canada. 2 feet (60 cm).

Luzula nivea. A fine white woodsedge. 15 inches (37 cm).

Luzula sylvatica 'Variegata'. N. Great woodrush. This makes good ground cover, and is nice when in flower in early summer. 1 foot (30 cm).

Lychnis flos-jovis. N. The pink ragged robin. Fine for naturalising beside a ditch. 1½ feet (45 cm).

Lysimachia punctata. Yellow loosestrife. Height 2 feet (60 cm), with spikes of yellow flowers in July. (The native *L. vulgaris* spreads much too fast).

Milium effusum 'Aureum.' Bowles's golden grass. Most useful garden foliage, and likes moisture.

Physostegia virginiana. Obedient plant. Its penstemon-like flowers (in September) swivel on their bases, and when moved stay put. 1½ to 2 feet (45–60 cm). (See p. 55).

Polygonum amplexicaule. Knotweed. A common, robust and useful plant, with deep red flower spikes in July. 6 inches (15 cm).

Polygonum miletti****.** Handsome crimson spikes 1 to 1½ feet (30–45 cm). From Nepal, where it grows right in water.

Polygonum sphaerostachyum***.** Another very graceful and showy knotweed of rich pink flowers from August onwards. 1 to 1½ feet (30–45 cm).

Primula spp***.** All the 'candelabra' types are suitable, especially *P. pulverulenta, P. japonica, P. prolifera, P. bulleyana, P. burmanica, P. beesiana* and many of their hybrids, e.g. Asthore Hybrids, Inshriach Hybrids. Also good is *P. sikkimensis*. Some will seed themselves freely, especially *P. pulverulenta*, and a few, like *P. prolifera* will flourish with their roots completely under water. Most of these flower in spring and early summer. They grow from 1 to 3 feet (30–90 cm).

Rodgersia aesculifolia and other spp. (See Section C).

Schizostylis coccinea and cultivars***.** A South African plant that is hardy and loves wet conditions. Very late flowering, from October onwards; red or pink. 15 inches (37 cm).

Stylophorum diphyllum. Celandine poppy. Even the bristly pendent seed pods are attractive, as are the foliage and big yellow flowers in May. 1 foot (30 cm).

Tradescantia virginiana. Spiderwort. A well-known herbaceous plant; many variations in flower colour of blue, pink, purple and white. 12 to 15 inches (30–37 cm). *T. brevicaule* is a smaller species with rosy purple flowers.

Tricyrtis hirta**.** Toad lily. Strange and interesting, and very late flowering (autumn); dull purple and spotted. 1 to 1½ feet (30–45 cm).

Polygonum sphaerostachyum, above, is not too invasive, unlike some other knotweeds; *Schizostylis coccinea* 'Sunrise', below, welcome for its late flowers and increasing freely

Cimicifuga racemosa, above, flowers in October and needs no support despite its height; *Campanula lactiflora* 'Prichard's Variety', below, with crowded heads of violet-blue bellflowers

Trollius europaeus******. N. Globe flower. The many cultivars and hybrids are some of the showiest and most important of all bog plants for May and June. 1 to 1½ feet (30–45 cm).

Trollius ledebourii******. Striking open flowers, not like globes; later flowering. Another valuable bog plant. 1 to 1½ feet (30–45 cm).

Section C: Larger plants for bold effects

Artemisia lactiflora. A handsome white-flowered wormwood with dark green foliage. 2½ feet (75 cm).

Aruncus sylvester. A useful white 'spiraea', especially the male plants; 3 feet (0.9 m). The cultivar 'Kneiffi' is a daintier version; 2½ feet (75 cm).

Campanula lactiflora. . Flowers from July onwards. The cultivar 'Prichard's Variety' is a specially good blue. 3 feet (0.9 m).

Cimicifuga spp****. Handsome foliage, and striking white spikes of flowers late in the year. 3 to 6 feet (90 cm to 1.8 m).

Cortaderia selloana*****. Pampas grass, which can be seen at its best in the National Trust garden at Sheffield Park in Sussex. 6 feet (1.8 m).

Eupatorium cannabinum. N. Hemp agrimony. The pink flowered species, common along our canals and riversides. 3 feet (0.9 m).

Eupatorium purpureum**. Joe Pye weed. A fine American background plant, with striking stems and foliage. Deep purplish red flowers in autumn. 6 feet (1.8 m).

Euphorbia palustris**. A big spurge that revels in damp soil and makes large clumps; flowers of the typical acid green. Beware the irritant milky juice. 3 feet (0.9 m).

Miscanthus sinensis 'Variegata', one of the most decorative taller grasses

Gunnera manicata**.** Prickly rhubarb. This vast plant from Chile has the largest leaves of any plant hardy in this country; it loves to grow in liquid mud. We usually thatch over the crowns in winter with a frost-protective layer of bracken, and then its own dead leaves to keep the bracken dry. 6 to 9 feet (2–3 m).

Gunnera chilensis***.** 3 to 6 feet (1–2 m), is a smaller species of similar appearance.

Iris ochroleuca. A stiffly upright plant; yellow and white. Flowers in late summer. 3 feet (0.9 m).

Lysichitum americanum*.** Another genus that loves to grow in liquid mud. Large bright-yellow arum flowers from early March onwards; allowance must be made for the huge leaves, up to 4 feet (1.2 m) long, that follow. It may seed itself.

Lysichitum camtschatcense**.** A choicer and smaller plant with pure white flowers in spring. 2 feet (60 cm).

Miscanthus sinensis cultivars**.** Handsome grasses that add so much to the aquatic scene, and are better behaved than some of the bamboos. 3 to 5 feet (0.9–1.5 m).

Peltiphyllum peltatum.** A vast "saxifrage", with early drumstick-like heads of pink flowers, and big leaves on 4½ feet (150 cm) tall stalks that seem to be imitating the gunneras. There is a fine dwarf cultivar, 'Nanum'*****, with rich autumn colour, 15 inches (38 cm).

The enormous leaves and flower spikes of *Gunnera manicata* emerge dramatically in spring

The bog arum, *Lysichitum americanum*, above, has brilliant yellow
flowers with an unpleasant scent; *Rheum palmatum* 'Rubrum', below,
useful where space allows for its bold leaves as well as flowers

Phalaris arundinacea 'Picta'. Gardeners garters. A common garden grass whose young foliage is of particularly bright variegation. It flowers in July. 2½ feet (75 cm).

Phormium tenax. New Zealand flax. This huge plant with large and remarkably tough, iris-like leaves, and towering brown flower spikes. 6 to 8 feet (1.8–2.4 m). There are now many smaller sorts, e.g. *Phormium cookianum*, and also purple leaved and variegated cultivars.

Polygonum campanulatum***. A most useful 'filler', where there is plenty of space; masses of pink flowers in autumn, and quite a shrub-like effect. It does not root deeply and is not a nuisance, as many of its relatives are, although it will cover a lot of ground quickly. 2–4 feet (60–120 cm).

Primula florindae*. 4 to 5 feet (1.2–1.5 m.) Yellow flowers borne in June to July; will flourish in water and form large clumps.

Rheum palmatum 'Rubrum'****. A large ornamental rhubarb, sometimes listed as 'Bowles's Variety,' with deeply-cut reddish leaves like that of rhubarb. When in flower (in June) it resembles a huge red astilbe; up to nearly 6 feet (1.8 m). (See p. 61).

Rodgersia aesculifolia and other spp***. Robust and opulent foliage, often with a bronzy tinge. Flowers in summer. 3 feet (0.9 m). (See page 10).

Spiraea filipendula. 'Magnifica' and 'Venusta' are two good pink flowering ones. 5 feet (1.5 m).

Symplocarpus foetidus. Skunk Cabbage. A real 'stinker'! It loves to grow in almost liquid mud. The flowers in February are hard to see; they are dark brown and at ground level. The largish leaves come later.

Thalictrum flavum. N. Meadow rue. Tall and robust with heads of yellow flowers in July–August. *Thalictrum glaucum* is the better of the two; big, with grey foliage and striking yellow flower heads. 4 feet (1.2 m).

Section D: Bulbs

Fritillaria meleagris***** N. Snakeshead fritillary. Our wild fritillary which used to be seen in wet meadows in vast numbers; the remnants are now carefully preserved. Very graceful, and will seed itself when suited in limy soil. 9 to 12 inches (23–30 cm).

Leucojum aestivum***. N. Summer snowflake. Flowering from April to June. 'Gravetye Giant' is a very large cultivar that can flourish even with its bulbs well below water level. 18 inches (45 cm).

Leucojum vernum***. Spring snowflake. The March-flowering snowflake is also a fine moisture lover. 6 inches (15–22 cm).

Section E: Ferns

Matteuccia struthiopteris***. Ostrich feather fern or shuttlecock fern, from the way the leaves spring out from the crown; it increases by sending its rhizomes through the wet soil. 1½ to 2 feet (45–60 cm).

Onoclea sensibilis. Sensitive fern. This fern loves the water's edge, and increases almost too fast once it gets established. 3 to 4 feet (0.9–1.2 m).

Osmunda regalis****. N. Royal fern. At its best when its roots go right down into the water, and the mat they make forms a fine stable edge to pond or ditch bank. 3 to 4 feet (0.9–1.2 m).

A group of astilbes, hostas and day lilies

Section F: Trees and shrubs

Many, like the willows, alders, poplars, aspens, birches and dogwoods, as well as some conifers, love moisture and can help to make a suitable background where there is enough room.

From the alders one gets winter catkins and the characteristic stalked buds; *Alnus incana* 'Aurea' has golden leaves, and also has remarkable pink catkins. The willows may have silvery leaves (*Salix lanata*) or coloured bark (*Salix alba* 'Chermesina'). Fine winter catkins grace *Salix daphnoides*, the violet willow, which makes a small tree and has a waxy 'bloom' on the young growth. If a smaller bush is required, *Salix wehrhahnii* is a suitable choice, growing to 6 to 8 feet (1.8–2.4 m) wide and high.

Poplars and aspens are hardly garden trees, but there are a lot of attractive birches. Dogwoods, too, with their coloured barks, (*Cornus alba* 'Sibirica') are wonderful when seen across, and reflected in, the surface of a lake.

The deciduous cypress, *Taxodium distichum* with its 'knees that breathe', likes to be on the edge of the water, and so does the dawn redwood, *Metasequoia glyptostroboides*.

INVASIVE PLANTS BELOW STAR CLASSIFICATION

This list is in addition to those mentioned earlier.
Cyperus longus, *Hydrocotile* spp., *Mentha* spp. especially *M. aquatica* and *M. gentilis*, *Petasites albus* and *P. fragrans*, *Polygonum sachalinense*, *P. cuspidatum* and *P. amphibium* (the first two are terrible pests). *Senecio tanguticus*, *Ulmaria vulgaris*, *Epilobium* spp., *Heracleum mantegazzianum*, *Houttynia cordata* and *H. cordata* 'Flore Pleno', *Montbretia* spp., *Lactuca (Mulgedium)* spp. *Phragmites communis*, *Scutellaria galericulata*, *Sparganum* spp., *Stachys palustris*, *Zizania latifolia*.

Ranunculus lingua 'Grandiflora' is an excellent plant for bog or shallow water if kept under control